Philosophy begins in wonder.
Plato, *Theaetetus* **155d**

Series 117

This is a Ladybird Expert book, one of a series of titles for an adult readership. Written by some of the leading lights and outstanding communicators in their fields and published by one of the most trusted and well-loved names in books, the Ladybird Expert series provides clear, accessible and authoritative introductions, informed by expert opinion, to key subjects drawn from science, history and culture.

The Publisher would like to thank the following for the illustrative references for this book:
Page 23 'Forms, copies and works of art' © Stephen Orsillo/Dreamstime.com

Every effort has been made to ensure images are correctly attributed, however if any omission or error has been made please notify the Publisher for correction in future editions.

MICHAEL JOSEPH

UK | USA | Canada | Ireland | Australia
India | New Zealand | South Africa

Michael Joseph is part of the Penguin Random House group of companies whose addresses can be found at global.penguinrandomhouse.com

Penguin
Random House
UK

First published 2019
001

Text copyright © Angie Hobbs, 2019

All images copyright © Ladybird Books Ltd, 2019

The moral right of the author has been asserted

Printed in Italy by L.E.G.O. S.p.A.

A CIP catalogue record for this book is available from the British Library
ISBN: 978–0–718–18852–8

www.greenpenguin.co.uk

MIX
Paper from responsible sources
FSC® C018179

Penguin Random House is committed to a sustainable future for our business, our readers and our planet. This book is made from Forest Stewardship Council® certified paper.

Plato's *Republic*

Angie Hobbs

with illustrations by
Angelo Rinaldi

Ladybird Books Ltd, London

Plato's world

Plato was born *c*. 428/427 BCE (possibly 424/423 BCE) into an aristocratic Athenian family at a turbulent time: throughout his youth the city-state (*polis*) of Athens was engaged in a brutal civil war with the city-state of Sparta. Though they had come together to defeat the threat from the Persian Empire at the beginning of the century, after the Persians were overcome in 480 the two great Greek powers and their allies vied for supremacy; hostilities broke out in 431 and lasted until Athens was defeated in 404. Athens was also divided internally during this period between supporters of a democratic system of government in which all adult male citizens participated directly and those who favoured an oligarchic system in which power was in the hands of a wealthy few. Plato himself had family connections to both factions, and the desire to avoid internal strife shaped his political thinking.

As an aristocrat Plato was destined for a stellar political career. Two things changed his course. The first was his disgust with the violent extremes of the oligarchic faction, particularly when they briefly came to power in 404. Then, when democracy was restored in Athens, it put to death his beloved friend and mentor Socrates, purportedly for refusing to believe in the city's gods and introducing new ones, and for corrupting the young. In grief and revulsion Plato abandoned a conventional political career for a life in philosophy, 'the love of wisdom'. After travels in Greece, southern Italy, Sicily and perhaps Cyrene and Egypt, in the 380s he set up a research and teaching institute, the Academy, just outside the Athenian city walls. Apart from two more trips to Sicily, he remained at the Academy for the rest of his life.

Plato's work

Plato's range is vast. He writes about ethics, political theory, psychology, aesthetics, knowledge and reality, and shows how he believes all these subjects interconnect. Probably inspired by Socrates' oral style, he almost always chooses to write in dialogue form: deploying a wide and vivid cast of characters, he never writes in his own voice, thus encouraging his readers to enter into the debate and engage in active interpretation for themselves. Although 'Socrates' is usually the main character, we cannot assume that Plato uncritically endorses everything he puts into Socrates' mouth – and Socrates' words are often challenged by highly intelligent interlocutors, as they are in the *Republic*; nor can we assume that 'Socrates' is the mouthpiece for the historical Socrates. With wit, verve and often detailed scene-setting, these dazzling works draw us into their richly imagined worlds.

The dialogue later called *Res Publica* by the Romans (*Politeia* in Greek) was probably written during the 370s, initially on wax tablets (there is a story that Plato experimented with many different versions of the opening sentence). It attracted immediate interest and papyrus copies were soon circulating freely around Athens; in the following century it appeared in the great library at Alexandria. It remained known – usually through references in Latin by authors such as Cicero – throughout the later classical world and the Middle Ages, and its readership expanded hugely in the fifteenth century when it was translated into Latin by the Florentine philosopher Marsilio Ficino. Its enduring appeal is explained in large part by its fundamental central questions: what is justice, and does it pay me personally to be just?

Plato standing by a bust of Socrates.

Layout of the *Republic*, and opening scene

Since at least the second century CE the *Republic* has traditionally been divided into ten books (although it is not clear that these divisions were made by Plato, who may have favoured six). Also in universal use is the referencing system to particular passages (such as 473c) derived from the sixteenth-century edition of the complete works of Plato by a French scholar known as Stephanus.

The dialogue opens with Socrates and one of Plato's brothers, Glaucon, going down from Athens to the harbour at Piraeus to witness the festival of the Thracian goddess Bendis, newly adopted by the Athenians. After seeing the procession and saying their prayers they are returning up to town when they are waylaid by a businessman, Polemarchus, and several of his friends, including another of Plato's brothers, Adeimantus. Polemarchus invites Socrates and Glaucon to join them all for discussion in his house nearby, where he lives with his father, Cephalus; he says that later in the evening they can all return to the festival to see a sensational torch relay on horseback in honour of the new goddess.

It is a vibrant and deft introduction to a number of themes that will run throughout the work. Given that one of the charges against Socrates at his trial was that he refused to believe in the city's gods and introduced new ones, it is telling that Plato subtly shows us that it is in fact the Athenians themselves who are introducing a new god. Socrates, though happy to pay conventional respects to Bendis, prefers philosophic discussion to watching most of the day's glamorous novelties: it is significant that there is no mention of him returning to see the torch relay.

First attempts to define justice:
Cephalus and Polemarchus

At Polemarchus' house, Socrates asks the wealthy old man
Cephalus what he thinks is the greatest advantage of being
rich. Cephalus replies that wealth makes it easier to be just and
do the right thing (the Greek word for 'justice' is rather broader
than the modern English term): money enables you to make
the appropriate sacrifices to the gods and, in your dealings
with your fellow men, it allows you the luxury of telling the
truth and returning what you have borrowed. Socrates protests
that these may not always be the right things to do: what if we
borrow a weapon from a friend who subsequently goes mad
and asks for it back? Surely it would not be right to return it?
Cephalus agrees, but has no interest in pursuing the discussion
about what justice really is – he has more sacrifices to make –
and hands over to his son Polemarchus.

Polemarchus claims that justice is giving others their due,
and this means helping one's friends and harming one's
enemies – the code of the heroes such as Achilles and
Odysseus in Homer's epic poems. But, says Socrates, can we
not be mistaken about who are our true friends and enemies?
Polemarchus admits this, and refines his definition to say that
justice is helping the friend who both seems and is good, and
harming the enemy who both seems and is bad. Socrates is still
not satisfied: surely it is not the part of the good, just man to
harm *anyone*?

With this move, Socrates repudiates the conventional code of
revenge; it is clear that his revision of justice is going to be
radical and new.

What is justice? Thrasymachus

At this point Thrasymachus bursts into the debate 'like a wild beast'. Thrasymachus is a sophist, one of the itinerant teachers of the art of persuasion who taught young men from wealthy families how to get ahead in public life, and Plato's portrayal of them is generally hostile. This is all sanctimonious nonsense, Thrasymachus says: justice is simply the interest of the stronger. In any state, whether a democracy, tyranny or anything else, whichever person or party is in power makes the laws in their own interest and calls obedience to these laws 'justice'; so the obedient subject is simply furthering the interest of those in power and is a fool to go along with it.

In response Socrates tries to convince Thrasymachus that any art, including the art of ruling, has the interests of its subject matter at heart, in this case the ruled. But Thrasymachus will have none of it. Rulers, he declares, are like shepherds: if they appear to care for their flock, it is only to fatten them up so that they can get a better price for them at market.

He then gives his second and full position: justice is treating other people decently and fairly while injustice is the ruthless promotion of one's own interests, conceived in terms of material wealth and power over others. It is injustice that pays the individual, not justice, and injustice that is the true virtue, the virtue of prudent good sense. We may despise the petty criminal, but when injustice is practised on a sufficiently grand scale, we admire it. We would all be tyrants if we could.

The historian Thucydides attributes similar views to some fifth-century BCE politicians and military commanders.

Glaucon and Adeimantus develop Thrasymachus' position

Socrates tries to argue that injustice leads to disunity and failure. But his arguments are unsatisfying, and Glaucon and Adeimantus step in to strengthen Thrasymachus' position.

For Glaucon, what we term 'justice' is simply a pragmatic social contract: I won't harm you if you don't harm me. But if we could do wrong undetected, we would. To support this, he tells the legend of Gyges' ring. Gyges, a poor Lydian shepherd, discovers in a chasm opened up by an earthquake a ring which renders its wearer invisible. Within a month he has utilized this magical power to kill the King of Lydia and marry the Queen.

Glaucon challenges Socrates to show that justice is better than injustice, irrespective of any consequences. Can Socrates prove that the just man leads a more flourishing life, even if he is wrongly accused of injustice and tortured and killed? And even if the unjust man is mistaken for a just person and lauded with honours and financial rewards?

Adeimantus adds that people only act justly if they can benefit from having a just reputation; the ideal is therefore to cultivate the reputation for justice while still behaving unjustly in secret. This cynical policy will win you the favour not only of men but also of the gods, who can be readily bought off: so 'sin first and sacrifice later from the proceeds'.

Can Socrates demonstrate that justice belongs to the highest class of goods, those that are worth having not only for their consequences but, much more importantly, for themselves?

The first, 'healthy' classless society

Socrates says that it will be easier to discover justice first on the larger canvas of a state, before seeing whether they can transfer their findings to the individual. Therefore they need to construct a state from scratch, and see how justice and injustice originate in it.

The fundamental cause of human association is economic: it would simply be too time-consuming for each individual to make and grow absolutely everything needed for survival, so there must be specialist farmers, builders, weavers, merchants, sailors, retailers and labourers. This division of production and supply also makes the best use of our different natural aptitudes. Socrates, Glaucon and Adeimantus are not yet clear about exactly where to find justice in such a community, but they believe it will exist somewhere in the mutual relations between these groups – although at this stage there is no mention of a political hierarchy. This proto-society appears to be anarchic, without political leaders.

Life will be pure, simple and rural: the people will lie on beds of myrtle and dine on a vegetarian diet of wine, barley-bread, cheese, figs and roasted acorns, served not on tables but on leaves. They will respect the gods and live within their means, thus avoiding both poverty and war. There is no mention of the fine arts, poetry or philosophy.

Is this proto-society just a mischievous parody of the contemporary literary fashion for imagining a mythical Golden Age (whether in the past or – as here – the future)? There are certainly elements of that, but Socrates does say clearly that this community is both 'true' and 'healthy'.

The second, ideally just but 'fevered' state

Glaucon, however, complains that this simple, classless society is nothing more than 'a community of pigs' (a sly reference perhaps to the roasted acorns?). Socrates acquiesces and says he will construct a more sophisticated, cultured society: there will be couches and tables; delicacies, perfumes, cosmetics, courtesans and confectionary; painting, poetry, music and theatre and luxury goods of gold and ivory.

But this society is now in the grip of 'unnecessary' desires – their satisfaction is not required for our physical survival – and such desires are also unlimited: the sophisticated society will desire more and more and no longer be healthy but bloated and 'feverish'. In the ceaseless quest to fulfil such desires it will seek to expand its territory to make room for all the new occupations (including more doctors for all the new ills) and this will anger its neighbours; war will result. The cause of war, declares Socrates, is thus the same as the cause of most evils: greed.

On the principle of job specialization already agreed on, there will now need to be a separate military class of Guardians to fight the inevitable wars that follow from the pursuit of unlimited desires. And this will require selecting those of suitable characteristics: fast; strong, spirited and courageous. But this gives rise to a serious challenge: how do you ensure that the Guardians are fierce against enemies but gentle to their own people? How do you guard the Guardians?

Primary education of the Guardians: censorship of the arts

The answer lies in a system of primary education which achieves the correct balance between two different elements of the psyche or personality: the rational, wisdom-loving ('philosophic') part and the spirited part, the *thumos* or *thumoeides*. This is brought about by the appropriate mix of education in the arts and physical education.

But much existing literature – Homer, for instance, and the tragic poets such as Aeschylus – is dangerous, for both theological and moral reasons. Firstly, it often inaccurately depicts the gods as cruel, violent, deceitful, lustful and capricious, meting out good and bad fortune indifferently to honourable and dishonourable people, whereas in fact god (the switch from plural gods to singular god is interesting) is entirely good and the cause only of good; evil in the world has some other origin. Secondly, poetry frequently describes and represents (representation is especially dangerous as it involves identification) immoral desires and disproportionate emotional responses in its heroes and thus fosters such faults in the humans who emulate them. Strict censorship will therefore be necessary.

The *Republic* gives notably more prominence to education than law in its prescriptions for the development of good citizens, and in making education a matter for state rather than private provision it goes against existing Athenian practice. Plato views young children as immensely impressionable and believes that it is vital that they internalize the rhythm and harmony of beautiful and moral art from birth.

The division of the Guardian class into two: Rulers and Auxiliaries

Some of the trainee Guardians are now selected to be future Rulers, with the rest serving as their Auxiliaries. There are thus now three classes in the state: Rulers, Auxiliaries and Producers (and almost certainly some non-Greek slaves). Myths are created to encourage all the citizens to regard each other as brothers from the same Mother Earth, and to accept that they naturally fall into three categories: gold, silver and iron/bronze.

These myths have given rise to two keen debates. Do they endorse racism? And to what extent are they deceptive propaganda? In respect of the first, it is important to note that promotion and demotion between classes is obligatory if children born into one class turn out to have the abilities suited to another. As for the second, the Greek terms could indicate either a deliberate lie or a community-binding story not intended to be taken entirely literally.

The Guardians (both Rulers and Auxiliaries) are to work for the good of the whole state and not for the good of any one class. To this end they are to live in communes where all their material needs are provided by the Producers; the Guardians themselves are not allowed any personal wealth or possessions. The Producers are allowed personal property, but extremes of wealth or poverty among them are prevented by state intervention.

The state as a whole will be wise through the wisdom of the Rulers, courageous through the courage of the Auxiliaries and temperate if all three classes agree that the Rulers should rule. Justice in the state will be the underlying condition that results in this social harmony, namely each class performing its proper function.

A Producer bringing supplies to an Auxiliary.

Justice in the individual

Justice is thus shown to be of clear benefit to the state. But Thrasymachus' challenge was whether justice benefits the *individual*. Can Socrates translate his findings about the tripartite just state to the individual person? This will partly depend on whether the individual psyche can be divided into three on similar lines to the state.

Socrates argues – controversially – that the existence of various types of mental conflict shows that it can. The individual psyche comprises reason, analogous to the Rulers; the spirited element (*thumos*), analogous to the Auxiliaries; and the appetites, analogous to the Producers. (This tripartite psyche later influenced Freud's division of the psyche into ego, superego and id.)

The individual will be wise if reason is in control, ruling for the good of the whole psyche; courageous if *thumos* supports the decrees of reason; temperate if all three parts agree that reason should rule; and, as in the state, justice will again be the underlying condition that makes all this possible, namely that each psychic faculty perform its own specific function. The just psyche will therefore be harmonious and flourishing as well as virtuous: it will be mentally *healthy*, and since mental health is at least as important as physical health, justice will benefit the individual as well as the state.

This is a radical reworking of justice. Justice no longer simply consists of external actions but is a profound internal state of the agent. However, equating virtue with mental health and vice with mental illness can provide troubling opportunities for cynical political and medical exploitation.

Our desires for truth, success and physical satisfaction.

Women in the workforce

Socrates will partly address these issues in Book 9. But first he returns to the way of life of the Guardians, and in particular to the role of women.

Guardian women are to perform the same jobs as Guardian men, and thus serve alongside them as Rulers and Auxiliaries. This is because the only difference between the sexes is that the 'man begets and the woman bears' children, and this one biological difference does not affect what jobs women can do (or what virtues they can display). Guardian women should thus receive the same education and training as men. Whether an individual woman should be a Ruler or Auxiliary (or indeed anything else) will depend on her natural ability: women differ in aptitudes just as men do.

The Guardian women have often been criticized by commentators for being 'masculine', but this may reveal more about the prejudices of the critics than of Socrates (or Plato). However, it is true that Socrates does not appear to be interested in the 'rights' of women (or indeed men): his concern is to actualize and harness the potential of women for the overall good of the state. And we should note that the ability of some women to function as Guardians depends on the support of women in the Producer class (and probably female slaves as well). There are also several disparaging remarks made about women throughout the dialogue: Plato perceives a marked gulf between women as they might be if properly educated and women as they are now.

Nevertheless, the radical nature of Socrates' proposals is striking: Athenian women did not occupy such roles. And Plato did allow women to attend his lectures at the Academy.

Abolition of the nuclear family

As all the Guardians are to live in camp communes, Guardian women have already been freed from the responsibilities of running an individual home. Nevertheless, how are they to serve as soldiers and rulers if they are preoccupied with raising their children? Socrates' solution is simple and brutal (although he does express doubts about it): the nuclear family is to be abolished. In a deliberate programme of eugenics (frequently and disturbingly phrased in the terminology of stock-breeding), Guardian women and men are to be brought together at state mating festivals, with the noblest among them being given the most enticing opportunities to reproduce. Guardian babies are to be removed from their mothers at birth and raised in state nurseries, so that all the Guardians will regard each other as potential family members (the dangers of incest are recognized, although the provisions to prevent it are decidedly sketchy).

The purpose of all these arrangements is to prevent mental distractions and divided loyalties: the Guardians should share in the joys and sorrows of all the other citizens. Socrates wants to construct a state in which people use the terms 'mine' and 'not mine' of the same things.

Socrates says he knows that his proposals about women and the abolition of the family will cause a stir, and he was right: this part of the *Republic* has provoked heated debate from Plato's day on. It has also been viewed as containing the seeds of both communism and fascism. It is certainly totalitarian: the individual citizen is viewed as a part of a greater whole just as a finger is part of the body.

Philosopher-Rulers

But how is this ideally just state to come into being and not just remain a dream?

> *The society we have described can never grow into a reality or see the light of day, and there will be no end to the troubles of states, or indeed ... of humanity itself, till philosophers become kings in this world, or till those we now call kings and rulers really and truly become philosophers.* (*Republic* **473c–d**)

Socrates makes it clear in 540c that there are to be Philosopher-Queens as well as Philosopher-Kings. But who are the philosophers, the lovers of wisdom?

The answer depends on Plato's belief that true reality lies apart from the world that we perceive with our senses. Philosophers are those who have apprehended and love what he calls the perfect, unchanging, eternal, non-sensible *Forms* of Goodness and Beauty and Justice and so on, and indeed of both animate and inanimate objects. What is it, for instance, that connects all the beautiful things and people in this world? The answer is a mysterious entity (mysterious not just to us but to Plato's own students and even in part to himself) called the Form of Beauty, which allows us to arrive at a concept of beauty. The Form itself, however, is more than the concept: it would exist even if there were no humans around to apprehend it.

The world we perceive through our senses is a mere shadowy copy of reality; it is the intelligible realm of the perfect Forms that is truly real. Rulers therefore should be *experts* in what is truly beautiful and good.

Argument for the Forms

The main argument Socrates offers for the existence of Forms is epistemological, that is, one based on the conditions believed to be necessary for knowledge to exist at all. He claims this phenomenal world of sense-experience cannot be *known* because it is fluctuating, and subject to different individual perspectives, whereas knowledge requires *stable* objects. This changing and subjective world can therefore only be an object of *opinion*, not of *knowledge*.

It follows that if knowledge is to exist *at all*, it must be of a different realm, separate from this world. And that realm, claims Socrates, is the intelligible realm of perfect, eternal, unchanging Forms, such as those of Beauty, Justice and the Good. He does not want to consider the possibility that there might be no secure knowledge of anything . . .

In constructing this key argument, utterly central to the dialogue, Plato is influenced by two earlier philosophers: Heraclitus, who believed that everything is in a state of becoming, that 'everything flows' like a river; and Parmenides, who held that contrary to appearances there is only unchanging, eternal Being. In Plato's view, the world we see around us is a world of many different objects that are constantly changing, and which appear differently to different people at different times, or from different vantage points. To discover that which is eternal and unchanging we need to turn to the intelligible realm of the Forms.

It is an arresting argument, but it can be challenged: perhaps knowledge and belief should be distinguished not in respect of different fields of objects but in terms of their respective *reliability*: knowledge is always true; opinion may be true or false.

The philosopher seeking truth beyond the world of flux.

Philosophers, sophists and alternative facts

Why is Plato so committed to the existence of knowledge? Why is he not prepared to countenance the possibility that humans might have to withhold judgement?

The answer partly lies in his distrust and dislike of the sophists, the professional teachers of skills in public speaking and debate (such as Thrasymachus). Throughout his work, Plato is particularly opposed to those who teach their students how to make the weaker argument appear the stronger, peddling tricks in argumentation for argument's sake rather than making an honest and collaborative effort to search for the truth. He is also alarmed by the claim of one of the most famous sophists, Protagoras, that there is no such thing as objective truth and that each human simply creates his own subjective version of what is and what is not – that each 'human is the measure' of all things. Questioning and examining purported 'facts' is fine and good and what a philosopher should do, but doing away with any possibility of agreed reality is, Plato believes, both wrong and dangerous.

In his view such sophists give philosophy a bad name, and philosophy and sophistry need to be clearly distinguished. Commitment to the objective – indeed absolute – truth of the Forms and to knowledge of the Forms is the way to do this. It is worth remembering that in the defence speech made by Socrates at his trial in Plato's *Apology* (whether or not it is a record of what the historical Socrates actually said), it is claimed that some of the hostility against Socrates in Athens arose from people mistaking him for one of the sophists that they believed were corrupting the minds of young men.

A sophist bewitches the crowd – but not Plato.

The Simile of the Cave

The contrast between the mortal world of shifting phenomena and the intelligible and divine realm of perfect and unchanging Forms is illustrated by the powerful Simile of the Cave. We are bound by the legs and neck in a dark cave, facing a wall; behind us is a fire and between the fire and our backs runs a curtain-wall above which puppets are mysteriously moved.

All we can see on the wall in front of us are the shadows of puppets, which we mistake for real objects, both animate and inanimate. But if we are painfully released from our shackles and forced up a tunnel into the bright world above, although at first we will be dazzled, we will in time adjust to the true objects there and eventually be able to gaze at the sun itself, and realize that before we were prisoners in a world of deceptive shadows. And those few who do get to look upon the sun are compelled to return to the cave and use their knowledge to improve the lives of those who dwell there.

We can now understand more fully the dialogue's opening scene. Socrates' physical descent from Athens to the Piraeus anticipates the intellectual descent of the Philosopher-Ruler from the sunlit realm of the Forms to the shadowy cave: the opening word of the *Republic*, *katebēn* ('I went down'), looks forward to the philosopher *katabas*, 'going down', in 516e.

The implications of the simile for education are profound. The task of the teacher is to turn the mind's eye of the pupil in the direction of the light; the acquisition of knowledge has to be an active and internal process which the pupil undertakes for her- or himself.

Illusions ancient and modern.

Higher education of the Philosopher-Rulers

After the primary education in the arts and gymnastics and two to three years more physical training, some young Guardians are selected for a further ten years of military service and mathematical studies comprising, in order: arithmetic; plane geometry; solid geometry; astronomy and harmonics. At the age of thirty they undergo further tests and those selected then undertake five years of dialectic, an exercise in pure thought using reasoned argument from first principles (not just the assumptions of mathematics), aimed at apprehension of the Forms. Then come fifteen years of practical military and administrative experience until finally, aged fifty, a few will be guided (it is, frustratingly, not said how) to a revelation of the Form of the Good: these are the fully fledged Philosopher-Rulers. They will use the Form of the Good as a pattern both for their own lives and for society as a whole.

The Form of the Good is a mysterious entity, and even Socrates' interlocutors in the *Republic* struggle to comprehend it. However, the focus on mathematics as the best preparation for dialectic does provide some assistance: for Plato, the objects of mathematics provide the perfect link between this world of the senses and the intelligible realm of the Forms – over the entrance to the Academy was the sign 'Let no one enter here who has not studied geometry'. He studied mathematics with the Pythagorean communities in southern Italy, and may well have been influenced by the discovery attributed to them that music could be mathematically notated: if something as beautiful as music could be expressed through ratios, then perhaps everything good and beautiful in the entire cosmos was a matter of numbers and numerical proportions?

Plato discussing the tetractys symbol with a Pythagorean community in southern Italy.

Degeneration: timocracy, oligarchy and democracy

Socrates next considers how both the ideally just state and corresponding ideal character may degenerate into a descending order of morally corrupt states and characters: his aim is to see whether wickedness really does lead to a happier life. Degeneration, he claims, is inevitable in all created things, and in the case of the ideally just state starts with mistakes in the timing of the mating festivals and the ensuing birth of ill-bred Guardian children, who will disregard the communal and austere principles of the ideal Guardians and seek to own private property; they will also mistreat the Producers, regarding them as serfs rather than as fellow citizens.

This ambitious, honour-loving society (timocracy) then makes the critical mistake of equating honour with material wealth and degenerates further into an oligarchy where riches rule. The oligarchs, however, just look after their own narrow class interests and the ignored populace rises up against them, and democracy is born.

The kind of democracy Plato has in mind is direct democracy, in which the electorate (in the case of Athens, adult male Athenian-born citizens) votes directly on laws and policies. He has no experience of the representational variety in common practice today, in which the electorate votes for representatives to decide on laws and policies on its behalf. In a brilliant satire of contemporary Athens, he depicts both the charms of democracy – varied, tolerant, free-spirited, colourful – and also its weaknesses (he had after all seen Athenian democracy put Socrates to death): chaotic, fickle and above all fragile and vulnerable to attacks both from without and from within.

Entertaining the crowds in democratic Athens.

Demagoguery to tyranny

But although Plato was no fan of direct democracy, he did think it greatly preferable to tyranny, of which he had had direct experience in Sicily at the court of Dionysius I in Syracuse. Disturbingly, he thought that democracy could easily be subverted into tyranny by an opportunistic populist leader (demagogue), rule by the people swiftly collapsing into manipulative leading of the people. Here too he had had direct experience of populist demagogues in Athens.

The demagogue, says Socrates, gains power by democratic means, claiming to be champion of the people and making wild promises; in particular he offers intoxicating quantities of the neat spirit of independence. Anyone who opposes him is labelled 'an enemy of the people' and exiled, imprisoned or killed. Such tactics naturally create genuine enemies and the demagogue quickly acquires a large bodyguard, and eventually a private army. External conflicts are also stirred up to keep the people in need of a strong leader.

It is also in the demagogue's interests to keep his people poor as well as fearful, and when they start to rebel, protesting that this is not why they voted him in, he attacks them too and the full-blooded tyrant is born.

All these debased states correspond to similarly degenerate types of character. Whereas the mind (psyche) of the philosopher is ruled by reason, that of the honour-loving character is dominated by his or her spirited element (*thumos*) and its desires for glory and success; while the psyches of the oligarchic, democratic and tyrannical characters are dominated respectively by a love of money, a haphazard series of different desires, and one overweening obsession.

The states and individual lives compared

As a result, contrary to accepted opinion, the unjust tyrant is in fact *least* able to do what he wants because he is enslaved to the most obsessive of his sick and unlimited desires. He cannot do what is best for him because he does not understand what this is. He does not know what constitutes a flourishing human life or how to achieve it.

The supremely just philosopher, however, has the most pleasant, flourishing and free life, because he or she has the experience, intelligence and reason to judge the different types of pleasure sought by the different types of character and is in a position to know that the pleasures of the philosopher in seeking and contemplating truth and reality are more *real* and lasting than the pleasures afforded by the search for worldly honours and power, or material wealth and the satisfaction of physical appetites.

This addresses the issue of whether Socrates has equivocated, namely, that he has simply reframed justice in terms of mental health, rather than considering whether it pays to treat others fairly and decently. Socrates could now argue that most crimes are committed out of anger or jealousy or greed or lust, which only happens when the spirited element or appetites are in control. When reason is in control, there will not usually be any incentive to do wrong.

Socrates' arguments in this passage raise questions. Is it true that the philosopher has full experience of all three types of life? Are philosophers really never tempted to do wrong? Does the notion of 'real' and 'unreal' pleasures (as opposed to real and unreal *causes* of pleasure) make sense?

Which element in us will gain control? The rational man, the spirited lion or the appetitive monster?

Forms, copies and works of art

The account of true reality allows Socrates to expand on his concerns with art. All the transitory objects of this world are simply imperfect representations or imitations of the perfect, eternal Forms. The craftsman copies the ideal Form of the couch in his mind's eye, and the artist merely copies the craftsman's copy. Works of art are thus far removed from reality, on a par with shadows and reflections, and artists have no real knowledge of what they represent and are not to be regarded as guides or teachers (as the eighth-century BCE epic poet Homer certainly was at the time, the *Iliad* and *Odyssey* being considered by most Greeks as founts of moral and practical knowledge).

Artists also represent, appeal to and foster dangerous, irrational emotions which should be left to wither and die. Whereas in Books 2 and 3 art was to be heavily censored, now in Book 10 almost all art is to be reluctantly banned until a true philosophic art emerges. Socrates says he has loved the poems of Homer since he was a boy, but nevertheless Homer is to be courteously escorted out of their ideal state. All that is to be allowed are hymns to the gods and paeans in praise of good men.

There is an intriguing tension between the views expressed by Socrates and the literary techniques of Plato the off-stage author. The *Republic* is a great work of art as well as a great work of philosophy, deploying vivid characterization and creating haunting myths. Furthermore, it would be *banned* from the ideally just state that Socrates describes, as it does not meet the censorship criteria! Plato the supreme artist and ironist cannot have been unaware of this ultimate irony.

Three kinds of couch.

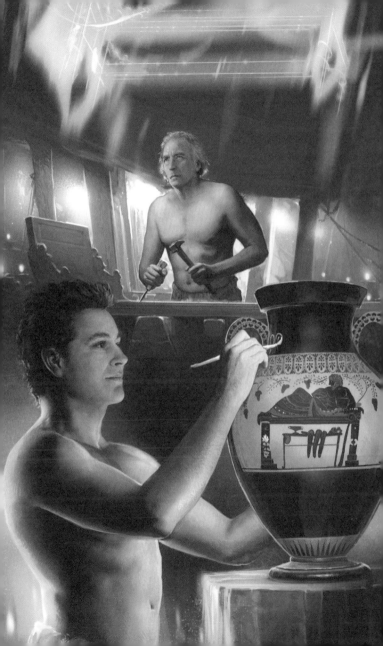

Rewards of the afterlife: the Myth of Er

Glaucon had challenged Socrates to show that justice pays the individual in terms of its intrinsic benefits rather than simply its consequences; Socrates now wants to portray the beneficial consequences as well. He believes he has shown that justice is a harmonious, healthy state of the psyche which comprises both virtue and flourishing and pays its possessor handsomely in this life. He now claims that the just person will also be rewarded after death.

To illustrate this, Socrates recounts (and partially invents) the Myth of Er. Er was a soldier killed in battle in Pamphylia (a region on the coast of modern Turkey) and his body was put on the funeral pyre. But before the fire was lit he came to life again and told of all that he had seen in the other world: horrific punishments for the unjust – especially tyrants – and wondrous rewards for the just. Souls transmigrate and how you live in this life shapes your choice of pattern of life for your next incarnation:

> *Excellence knows no master; a man shall have more or less of her according to the value he sets on her. The fault lies not with God, but with the soul that makes the choice.* (***Republic* 617e**)

Justice pays us in this life and the next, and if we remember this, all shall go well with us.

Part of Plato's project in the *Republic* has been to rework the notion of the divine and our relation to it, and the concluding moral of the Myth of Er is profound and radical: our good or ill fortune in both this life and the next is not due to the actions of capricious gods but is our responsibility. Our lives and afterlives are in our hands.

Afterlife of the *Republic*

The *Republic* has influenced, whether directly or indirectly, almost every philosopher since. But its reach extends far beyond philosophy. Plato has been called the father of both communism and fascism (the *Republic* was, for example, studied by Marx), and prominent twentieth-century critics of totalitarianism, such as Karl Popper and Isaiah Berlin, take issue with it (although their readings are very selective).

Its tripartite psychology influenced Freud, and poets have found inspiration in Plato's Theory of Forms and his depiction of our everyday world of sense perception as illusory; the film *The Matrix* adapts the Simile of the Cave in its chilling portrayal of humans unwittingly trapped in a fake reality.

But perhaps the chief reason for the dialogue's abiding appeal is that it asks such probing and universal questions – even if Socrates' solutions seem too extreme. Why should I be virtuous when vice so often appears to pay dividends? Why do humans form societies in the first place and what is needed for a society to thrive? How can women's potential be actualized? Is art ever dangerous, and if so, should there be any censorship by the state or should the dangers be allowed to remain in the interests of free expression? Do we want those in political charge to be experts at anything, and if so, what? How can democracies be protected from subversion by demagogues and tyrants?

These are some of the questions that seem particularly relevant in the early years of the twenty-first century. However, the *Republic* is so rich that each generation will be able to find something in it which can illuminate the challenges it faces.

Marx, More, Freud, Murdoch and Berlin have all responded to Plato's *Republic* – some more favourably than others.

Further reading

Plato, *Republic*, translated by Desmond Lee with an introduction by Melissa Lane (Penguin, 2007)

Julia Annas, *An Introduction to Plato's Republic* (Clarendon Press, 1981)

Melvyn Bragg and guests, *In Our Time: Plato's Republic* (BBC Radio 4, 29 June 2017, https://www.bbc.co.uk/programmes/b08vwn6h)

G. R. F. Ferrari (ed.), *The Cambridge Companion to Plato's Republic* (Cambridge University Press, 2007)

Angela Hobbs, *Plato and the Hero: Courage, Manliness and the Impersonal Good* (Cambridge University Press, 2000)

Iris Murdoch, *The Fire and the Sun: Why Plato Banished the Artists* (Clarendon Press, 1977)

Malcolm Schofield, *Plato* (Oxford University Press, 2006)

D. J. Sheppard, *Plato's Republic* (Edinburgh University Press, 2009)